Nicholas and His Neighbors

Written by Christopher A. Lane
Illustrated by Sharon Dahl

A SonFlower Book

VICTOR BOOKS®

A DIVISION OF SCRIPTURE PRESS PUBLICATIONS INC.
USA CANADA ENGLAND

Dedicated
to my son, Micah Benjamin.
The apple of my eye.

KIDDERMINSTER KINGDOM TALES
King Leonard's Celebration
Sir Humphrey's Honeystands
Nicholas and His Neighbors
Cornelius T. Mouse and Sons

DA EC

1 2 3 4 5 6 7 8 9 10 Printing/Year 94 93 92 91 90

ISBN: 0-89693-843-3
90-198397

VICTOR BOOKS
A division of SP Publications, Inc.
Wheaton, Illinois 60187

Nicholas and His Neighbors

In the Kingdom of Kidderminster, where King Leonard was king, there was once a village called Pupland nestled in a beautiful green valley. Down its quaint cobblestone streets trotted every sort of dog imaginable. There were large, handsome dogs who wore attractive coats and smart belts; short, snooty dogs who came from purebred families and wore tight, ruffled collars and fancy gloves; and even fat, shaggy dogs who wore spectacles and tall top hats.

One resident, however, stood out from all the rest. His name was Nicholas, and he lived all by himself. He was not handsome, snooty, or shaggy, and he did not wear smart belts, fancy gloves, or tall top hats. In fact, he looked unlike any of the dogs in all of Pupland.

You see, Nicholas was a cat.

His many brothers and sisters lived with his mother and father in a big house in the town of Pussywillow. They all had attended cat college and were now prominent doctors and lawyers. At first, his family thought farming a strange occupation for a cat. Farmers had little time for afternoon tea parties or naps in the sun. But Nicholas loved farming and had bought one of the good fields around Pupland. Having dogs for neighbors didn't bother him.

Having a cat for a neighbor did, however, bother the citizens of Pupland. In their opinion, Nicholas did not fit in. "His ears are too short and his tail too long," they said.

One dog in particular disliked Nicholas. His name was Ned, and he was the sheriff of Pupland. Ned was a large, strapping boxer who wore a blue hat and a sharp blue uniform which showed off his muscles. He strutted about town with a shiny gold star on his chest and made sure that no one broke the law.

Ned first noticed Nicholas on a quiet Friday afternoon. Ned was relaxing in the village square, watching the townsdogs pass by, when he heard a strange noise. It sounded like someone singing. As it grew louder, he noticed a farmer rolling a cart full of vegetables down the cobblestone street.

As the cart approached, Ned suddenly realized that the farmer was not a dog, but a cat. Leaping to his feet, he rushed to block Nicholas' path. "Where do you think you're going, cat?" Ned asked in a low growl.

"Why, good day, sir," Nicholas replied happily. "I'm on my way to market."

"Not here, you're not," the sheriff said, baring his fangs.

"But, sir, these vegetables are from my farm," Nicholas explained. "I've brought them to sell to the townsdogs."

"Pack 'em up and go back to your cat friends!"

"But I thought that this was a free town, sir, a place where both dogs and cats could live. You of all folks should know the law."

Nicholas was right. There was no law against cats living in Pupland. The two animals stared long and hard at each other until Ned growled and stepped aside.

"Go ahead, peddle your goods!" Ned called after him. "No dog will buy vegetables from a cat! And knock off that infernal singing!"

At the end of each week, the story was the same. Nicholas would bring his produce to market and Ned would pester him. He would encourage his buddies to bark and snarl at Nicholas, calling him names like "scaredy-cat" or "prissy puss." But rather than cry or run away, Nicholas would just turn his head and keep rolling his rickety cart slowly down the cobblestone street.

Early one summer morning, Nicholas was out in his field tilling the soil and singing a cheerful tune. He was especially happy because he was about to go to a family reunion near Pussywillow. He missed his family very much and was excited about getting to see them all once again.

On this day, Ned the Sheriff was also going on a trip. He was attending a meeting of the "Be Mean to Cats Association" in the nearby town of Poochville. Dogs from all over the countryside were attending, and since Ned was the treasurer for the group he was in charge of bringing the piggy bank. After packing his suitcase, he put on his hat and coat, checked to make sure that the piggy bank was full of dog biscuits, and set out for the convention down the Poochville Highway.

As he walked along thinking about all the fun he would have at the convention, Ned noticed that he was passing by Nicholas' farm. Spying the cat working in his field, he suddenly had a mischievous idea. "Well, look what we have here," he said with a sinister smile. "I think I have time enough to stop and see my old buddy Nicholas."

Setting aside his bag and piggy bank, Ned quietly made his way toward the cat. Sneaking up behind Nicholas, the boxer let out a bellowing bark.

Nicholas was so startled that he dropped his hoe and jumped high into the air, losing his hat and landing in a nearby stack of hay.

"Well, good morning, Mr. Nicholas!" Ned chuckled. "Rather jumpy today, aren't we? I'd love to stay and chat, but I must be on my way. I have an important meeting to attend. I'm sure you understand."

With a big grin across his face, Ned walked back, took up his bag and piggy bank and continued on his way toward Poochville.

"That dog . . . " Nicholas sighed, brushing himself off. "Just look at my clothes!"

Nicholas was upset, but not for long. He soon remembered his family reunion and cheered right up. And when his chores were done, he changed into his best overalls and hat and donned a brand-new bandana. He loaded his cart full of fresh vegetables to share with his family, packed some snacks in a knapsack, and took one last look at his map.

"North, up the Poochville Highway," he read, following the map with his paw. "Turn left at the Dog Tired Inn, up the hill and around the bend." It would take almost the whole rest of the day.

Nicholas closed the big wooden door of his red barn and began his journey. Upon reaching the entrance to the Poochville Highway, he paused to read a sign posted by the side of the road.

"Beware of Thieves," he read. "Hmm. I certainly hope there are no thieves out today."

Ned by now was ahead of Nicholas on the Poochville Highway. He knew that it was dangerous, but he was not afraid in the least. Even if he did meet up with any bad characters, he was confident that he could take care of them with one paw tied behind his back.

Now, it just so happened that a pack of wild dogs was planning an ambush. Their leader, a sleek black Doberman named Sid, had already devised a devious scheme. At his side, Mugsy, a small, energetic miniature collie, and Bruno, a huge St. Bernard, readied themselves for action. Camouflaged behind a row of thick bushes on the Poochville Highway, these ruffians waited to take advantage of some unwary animal.

"What do you see, Sid? What do you see?" Mugsy asked.

"Nothing," Sid replied, peering through a pair of binoculars in search of a worthy victim. "Hold it. Here comes someone."

"Huh? Someone's comin'!?" Mugsy yelped, bouncing up and down like a basketball. "You want me to go grab 'em? Huh? Do ya, Sid? Do ya?"

"Knock it off, Mugsy!" Bruno barked.

"Hey, I was just trying to be helpful," Mugsy began. "That's more than I can say for you, Bruno. You big, good-for-nothin' lug!"

"Come here, you little rat!" Bruno demanded, swiping at Mugsy with an enormous paw.

"Missed me, ya big lug!" Mugsy teased.

"You two knock off the chatter!" Sid ordered. "Now, you guys know the routine. Let's do it. He'll be here in a couple minutes."

The one Sid had spotted was none other than Ned, the sheriff of Pupland.

Bruno and Mugsy silently took their places as Ned came by.

"Excuse me, sir," Mugsy whined as he emerged from the bushes. "Can you spare a small biscuit for a hungry dog?"

"Ah, yeah, I guess," Ned replied, surprised at seeing the dog appear out of nowhere. After rummaging through his suitcase for a moment, he tossed Mugsy a couple of biscuits. "There ya go."

"Thanks," Mugsy grinned.

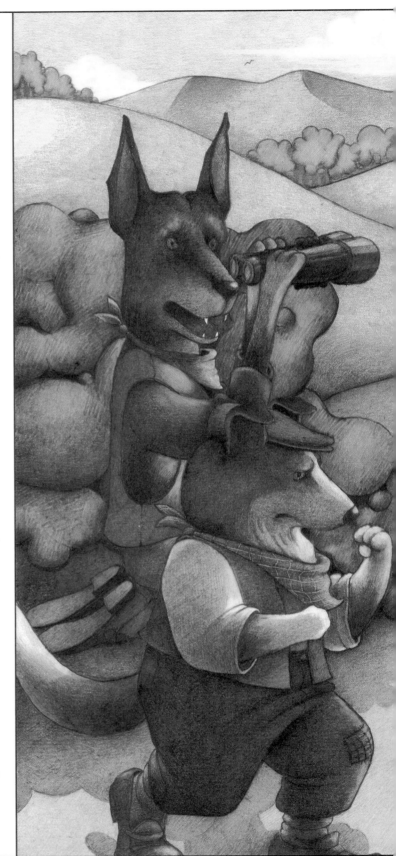

Then, just as Ned was about to pick up his luggage and continue on, Bruno leaped out from the bushes and grabbed the boxer. Before Ned could shake loose, Sid thumped him over the head.

"Good job, boys!" Sid said. "He won't be going anywhere for a while. Mugsy, get his hat. Bruno, grab his coat. I'll get his bag—and let's see what's in the pig."

Sid bashed the large bank against a nearby rock, and all three dogs gasped as they watched hundreds of dog biscuits pour forth.

"Wow! Look at all the biscuits!" Bruno bellowed.

"Yeah! We're rich! We're rich!" Mugsy yipped.

"You said it, boys," Sid agreed, licking his jowls.

Suddenly there was a noise like a twig breaking beneath someone's paw. Sid's ears perked up. "Shh. What was that?" he asked with his paw to his ear.

"What was what?" Bruno wondered. "I don't hear nothin'."

"Ha! You couldn't hear it thunder, ya big lug," Mugsy yipped.

"I've had it with you, ya little pipsqueak!" Bruno barked, swiping at Mugsy.

"Quiet!" Sid yelped. "Someone's coming! Quick, help me get the biscuits into this bag."

The three thieves loaded up the loot and hurried off into the bushes, leaving Ned unconscious beside the road.

Coming down the Poochville Highway was a terrier by the name of Dr. Scotty. He was a talented doctor who specialized in treating common dog ailments like fleas around the collar, crooked tail, and dry nose. Today Dr. Scotty was on his way to Poochville to perform an operation on a labrador who had stepped on his own tongue.

As Dr. Scotty rounded the bend, he was surprised to see a dog lying battered and bruised beside the highway. "Well, I'll be a leprechaun!" he exclaimed. "There's something lying by the road up ahead!" Carefully he moved in for a closer look. "Why, I do believe it's a dog. A boxer, in fact," he said, staring at Ned. "My, but he doesn't appear to be well at all. I'd better not get too close. Wouldn't want to catch anything."

Retreating to the opposite side of the road, Dr. Scotty wondered what he should do. "I suppose I should help him," he thought aloud. "But, my, look at the time," he said, glancing down at his watch. "I'm already running late for my operation! Perhaps I'll send my nurse back to tend to him. Yes, that's what I'll do."

So Dr. Scotty continued on his way toward Poochville, leaving Ned lying hurt on the side of the road. But as he walked on down the highway, he quickly forgot all about the injured boxer. By the time he reached Poochville, Dr. Scotty didn't even remember to send his nurse.

Some time later another traveler came along. It was Prissy Highnose, a poodle from a wealthy family, on her way to a prestigious dog show. Prissy's limousine had had a flat tire, and she had decided to go on ahead while her chauffeur attended to it. All decked out in an outfit which showed off her naturally curly hair, she hurried along so as not to miss the show. Rounding the bend in the road, she spotted Ned.

"Oh, my! How dreadful!" Prissy exclaimed. "Some poor creature has fallen by the roadside. I suppose someone should help him, but I surely wouldn't want to get all mussed up. I would just die if I soiled this new outfit!"

Standing across the road, the snooty pooch looked over at Ned. "He does appear to need assistance," she said thoughtfully. "But there is a chance that he is simply pretending to be hurt in order to draw me to his side. It is quite possible that he is a thief, waiting to steal my valuables. The cad! I simply won't fall for his trickery." She lifted her nose high into the air. "How distasteful. I knew I should've waited for my chauffeur Smedly to escort me to the show in the limousine."

And she continued down the road, never thinking of the injured dog again.

It was late afternoon when an overall-clad traveler pushing an old cart finally happened down the road. It was Nicholas the cat. By now he was over halfway to the family reunion and was getting more excited with each step. As he walked along, anticipating all the fun he would have, he made up a song:

What a jolly, joyful time
As we meet to hug and dine!
Telling stories and playing games
Trying to remember aunties' names.
Uncles, grandpas, brothers, cousins,
There'll be relatives by the dozens.
Clasping paws and swapping tales
Sharing love that never fails.

As his cart slowly rounded the bend in the road, Nicholas saw the large dog lying in the ditch up ahead.

"Uh, oh, thieves hereabout," he said wearily. "That unfortunate dog must have fallen prey to them. I wonder . . . should I stop to help him? It will be dark soon, and this highway is certainly not the place for a cat to be at night. And it could make me miss my family reunion. Besides, there is always a chance that this is some sort of trap," he thought aloud, peering into the bushes. "Perhaps this dog plans to rob me."

Then Nicholas shook his head. "No, those are silly excuses. This poor animal needs my help. Besides, it's the sort of thing I've heard good King Leonard would do."

Leaning over the injured dog, Nicholas
suddenly recognized him. "Why, it's
Ned!" he yelped. "And he's been robbed!
Let's see . . . I can use my bandana as a ban-
dage, and I have a little milk. I was saving it
for dinner, but Ned needs it much more
than I do."

Nicholas carefully bandaged Ned's
wounds and put drops of milk on his dry
tongue. After straining to load him onto
his cart, he summoned all of his strength to
continue pushing the cart down the road.

Fortunately, it wasn't long before they
reached the Dog Tired Inn. Nicholas
parked the cart.

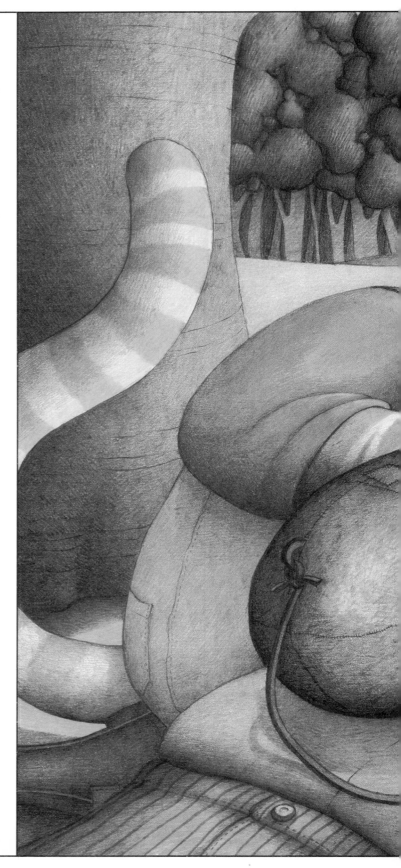

"Excuse me," he called out, ringing the bell at the front desk. "Hello? Is anyone here?"

"Yes, yes, I'm coming," a voice replied from the back room. "Keep your fur on!"

An elderly beagle waddled out and jumped up to the desk. "Now," he said, cleaning his spectacles, "what can I do for you?"

"Could I please rent a room, sir?" Nicholas asked politely.

The beagle sniffed and adjusted his glasses before responding. "Very well. Your name?" he asked, looking up at Nicholas for the first time. "Oh, my!" he said.

"Is something wrong, sir?" Nicholas asked.

"Wrong? Well . . . it's just that—we don't get many . . . I mean, you're— you're a—"

"A cat. Yes, I know."

"It doesn't make any difference to me, mind you, but . . . " The beagle paused, pointing to a sign near the door.

"No Cats Allowed," Nicholas read aloud. "Oh, I see. But, sir, I desperately need a room for the night. You see, I have a hurt dog outside in my cart."

"A hurt dog?" the clerk asked, glancing out the window. "Well, then, that changes things, doesn't it? Have you any biscuits?"

"Biscuits?" Nicholas questioned.

"Yes, dog biscuits. You know, money," he explained.

"Oh. No, sir, not a one. I do have fresh vegetables, though."

"Hmmm. This is highly irregular," the beagle said, rubbing his jowls. "But perhaps we can work something out."

Nicholas finally convinced the innkeeper to give him a room, and then helped Ned into bed. The injured boxer was unconscious through the rest of the afternoon and then all night, too. It wasn't until late the next morning that he came to.

"Where am I?" he grumbled groggily, wiping his eyes with his paws. "What's going on?"

"I'm glad to see you're awake," Nicholas said brightly. "You missed breakfast, but here's your lunch," he said, handing Ned a tray full of food.

"What are you doing here!?" Ned asked in surprise, rising up from the bed. "Ouch!! Oh, my head. What happened?

"I'm afraid you were robbed, Ned," Nicholas said sadly.

"I've got to get to that convention," the dog said, trying to stand. But he fell back on the bed.

"You're not going anywhere for a few days," Nicholas said.

"How did I get here?" Ned groaned. "Why are you here?"

Nicholas pulled a chair up next to Ned's bed. "I was on my way to a park near Pussywillow for a family reunion and found you lying beside the road."

"You mean, you helped me?"
Nicholas nodded.

"But what about all the mean things I've done to you? Trying to run you out of Pupland? Barking at you, pestering you?"

"We're still neighbors," Nicholas said, fiddling with his whiskers, "even if we don't always get along."

"Neighbors, huh?" Ned grunted. "I'm not exactly fond of cats. But you helped me."

"And you're welcome," Nicholas said. "Now, eat your lunch before it gets cold. I've got to get back to my farm. I have crops to tend to. You rest up and I'll be back to check on you in a few days."

Nicholas paid the innkeeper with the produce from his cart and asked him to take good care of Ned. As he pushed his now-empty cart down the Poochville Highway, a kitten-like smile crossed his face. It wasn't long before he began to sing.

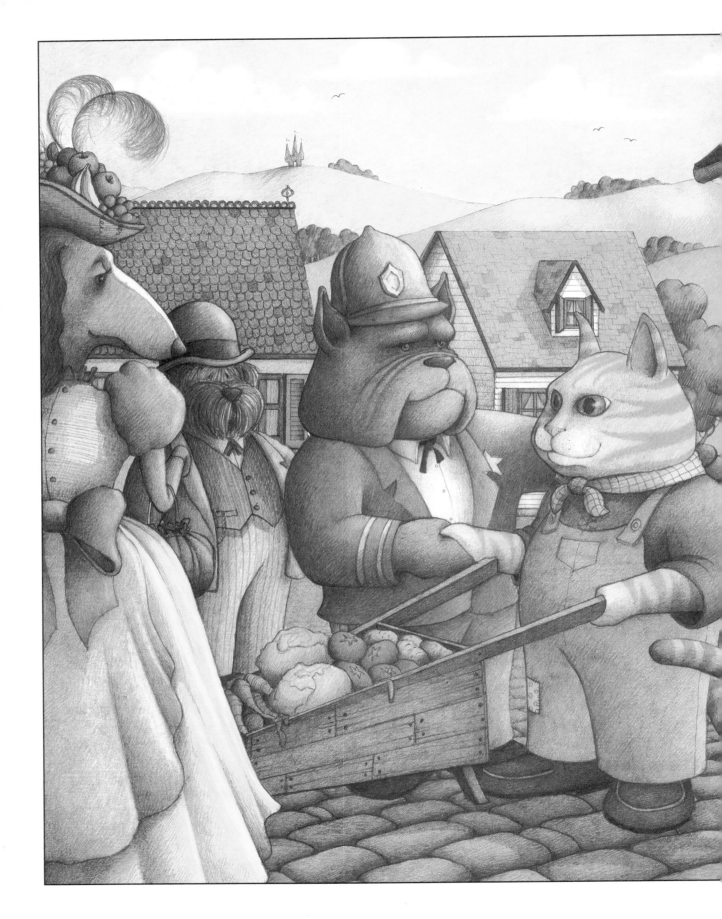

A few days later, Nicholas went back to check on Ned. The boxer was doing much better and felt well enough to return home. Nicholas invited Ned to stay in his barn until he was strong enough to return to his job as sheriff of Pupland.

Ned agreed, and in the coming days the two very different animals became friends. When Ned did return to work, he was a changed dog. He still wore his blue hat and sharp blue uniform which showed off his muscles. He still strutted about town with a shiny gold star on his chest and made sure no one broke the law.

But each Friday, when he heard someone singing and saw an overall-clad figure rolling his cart full of vegetables down the cobblestone street, he didn't leap up to block his path. Instead, he rose and cleared the way for the farmer cat.

"Make way, you dogs!" he would yell. And when Nicholas had brought his cart to a halt in the village square, Ned would announce his arrival. "Gather around, townsdogs! Come and see the fine vegetables of our neighbor, Nicholas the cat!"

The End

You can read a story like this in the Bible. Jesus told it in Luke 10:25–37:

On one occasion an expert in the law stood up to test Jesus. "Teacher," he asked, "what must I do to inherit eternal life?"

"What is written in the Law?" he replied. "How do you read it?"

He answered: " 'Love the Lord your God with all your heart and with all your soul and with all your strength and with all your mind'; and, 'Love your neighbor as yourself.' "

"You have answered correctly," Jesus replied. "Do this and you will live."

But he wanted to justify himself, so he asked Jesus, "And who is my neighbor?"

In reply Jesus said: "A man was going down from Jerusalem to Jericho, when he fell into the hands of robbers. They stripped him of his clothes, beat him, and went away, leaving him half dead. A priest happened to be going down the same road, and when he saw the man, he passed by on the other side. So too, a Levite, when he came to the place and saw him, passed by on the other side. But a Samaritan, as he traveled, came where the man was; and when he saw him, he took pity on him. He went to him and bandaged his wounds, pouring on oil and wine. Then he put the man on his own donkey, took him to an inn, and took care of him. The next day he took out two silver coins and gave them to the innkeeper. 'Look after him,' he said, 'and when I return, I will reimburse you for any extra expense you may have.'

"Which of these three do you think was a neighbor to the man who fell into the hands of robbers?"

The expert in the law replied, "The one who had mercy on him."

Jesus told him, "Go and do likewise."